E
Evincepub
Publishing

Evincepub Publishing

Nehru Nagar, Bilaspur, Chhattisgarh 495001
First Published by Evincepub Publishing 2021

ISBN: 978-93-5446-249-8

POETRY CELEBRATING THE WORKS OF GREAT ARTISTS

WRITTEN BY

DIBYASREE NANDY

ABOUT THE BOOK

Paying tribute to famous artists such as Claude Monet, Vincent Van Gogh, Edouard Manet, Hiroaki Takahashi, Rembrandt, Paul Cezanne, Pierre-Auguste Renoir, Edgar Degas, Toshi Yoshida, Paul Gauguin, Goya and others; I have written a hundred original poems describing selected artworks of each painter. I have mentioned the names of the paintings below every untitled poem of mine. The cover art is drawn by me, depicting Lachhmanjhula, Hrishikesh; the place I visited in early March last year.

"Choose only one master-nature." – Rembrandt

CONTENTS

CLAUDE MONET

Reflections of white pillars;
The glassy canal shimmers;
Trains chug along, puffing out fumes;
Near the embankment, a sailboat looms;
Grass and sand blend;
With heavy clouds the sky is bent;
Two men await a ride;
The wind shall serve as their guide.

-(The Railway Bridge at Argenteuil,
1873)

Nearly falling apart;
A rickety window pane, no one on alert;
Entangled by shrubbery;
Birds on the trees chirp, merry;
The blue pond, glittering jade;
Sultry afternoons soon fade;
Church in the far distance;
Standing tall, unwavering stance.

-(House by a pond, August 1856)

Ducks and cows, traipsing about;
The large pool with many a trout;
Barns with hay;
On a cool October day;
Buckets of water in the farmer's hands;
Son, an apprentice, soon to trim the lands;
Clumps of trees, an enclosure they form;
High, high, guardian against a storm.

-(Farmyard in Normandy, 1863)

Mahogany desktop cluttered;
The painted backdrop, a cave hidden, whispered
and muttered;
A red rug, velvety;
Dark green swirls adorn, pretty;
Leather-bound journals stacked;
A wooden box, with brushes and palettes 'tis
packed;
Rifle dark brown, crossed with a dagger pewter;
Hanging from the wall, protecting the sacred
altar.

-(Corner of a Studio, 1861)

Emerald and trailing;
Delicate to the touch, the lady twirling;
A cape shrouding her shoulders;
Her pensive face, the skin smoulders;
Soft fur at the rim;
A head-dress… with flowers they brim;
Dark brown stripes on green;
In the darkness, a fine sheen.

-{Camille (Woman in the green dress),
1866}

A grey-golden twilight sky;
Migratory birds fly;
Layers of crisp, pristine snow;
At dusk, softly they glow;
A shadowy cart forms a track;
The wheels clatter and clack;
Boughs silvery with rime;
With winter's melody, their journeys
rhyme.

-(Cart, Road under snow, near Honfleur, 1865)

Smothered by orange, yellow, red;
A spot of sunlight, a gentleman sat, a peony
bed;
Ships lining the sapphire sea;
The wind ruffles the flags with glee;
Parasols held aloft, couples socialize;
Smoke from the vessels rise;
The indigo azure, waves lap against boats;
Amidst the greenery of the flat roof, white are
the ladies' coats.

-(The Terrace at Sainte-Adresse, 1867)

A child with a spoon and plate;
Food on the tablecloth laid;
Two ladies sat, a maid in a white cap;
Bread, eggs and rolls, fish with chips, the blue
curtains flap;
A doll fallen under a chair;
Behind the veil, the gloved woman fair;
Folded newspaper, goblets full;
The bib… her caretakers straighten and
pull.

-(Luncheon, 1868-1870)

Black silhouettes, inky ripples on the lake;
A round patch of land in the midst, a picnic
with a cake;
Boats moored upon aquamarine;
Under a conical shelter, plenty of folks seen;
An ochre bank afar;
Olive foliage gently stir;
Bathers enjoy… waterscape filled with activity;
The dark shadows hum a
ditty.

-(La Grenouillere, 1869)

Hat upon the grass;
Watchful is the young lass;
Shades cast by the old trees;
The wind darts past… the silent river it frees;
Image of a white-washed house frowns on the
blue;
Innocent, the brook; without a clue;
At the dip of a valley runs the rill;
The opposite embankment, residents
fill.

-(On the bank of the river, Bennecourt, 1868)

VINCENT VAN GOGH

An expansive inn glum;
Ivy and creepers ripe with plum;
A murky sky, brown and grey;
Infinite droplets of rain yet to join the fray.
Tables and pillars white;
The coats of the customers olive and bright;
Where eyes can gleam hearing gossip;
As tea and wine they sip.

-(Restaurant de la Sirene; 1887)

A metal vase, dull gold;
It sat upon a wooden table old;
Blossoms of orange, downturned petals;
Leafy blades flowing out, splotches of
emeralds.
Dotted with indigo, flecked with shades of
green;
The wall behind, not quite clean;
Vermillion floral fringe;
A couple threatening to wilt and cringe.

-(Crown Imperials in a Copper Vase; 1887)

A bearded gentleman in a straw hat;
In a snug blue suit, he was clad;
Arms folded, resting upon trousers brown;
Features marred by a slight frown.
The walls depicted a village of snow;
Peach boughs seem to glow;
A summit adorned by flowers crimson;
Pathway curved, a lovely lady walks, hair in a
bun.

-(Portrait of Pere Tanguy; 1887)

Slanting yellow roofs, lantern underneath;
People gathered around tables beneath;
A waitress in white served;
Dark green branches swayed and curved.
Shops lit, houses at night, couples passed by;
Evening explodes with golden orbs in the sky;
Above the eatery, windows open;
The diner door near the cobbled lane.

-(Café Terrace on the Place du Forum; 1888)

Swirls of white amidst the palest of sapphires;
Barns and chimneys against the sky like spires;
A meadow sparkling like jade;
The yellow harvest seems to fade.
Blue and green, many a bush;
A tall tree dark, silences the fields with a shush;
Winds twirl by fast;
A spell of softness is cast.

-(Green Wheat Field with Cypresses; 1889)

Black, brown, grey branches;
The pink of the flowering trees dances;
A farmer works in the afternoon glare;
The reds of the roofs nearby flare.
As young olive shrubs flourish;
If you appreciate not this town of fruits, you're
foolish;
Blades of budding orange twist upwards;
The tall building afar, glances at the hues
downwards.

-(Orchard in blossom with view of Arles;
1889)

Gnarled trees streaked with black and brown;
Lush is the leaf's crown;
A man in its shelter as autumnal grasses sway;
Gloomy is the honey-hued building along the
pathway.
'Tis but a prison, the sky is about to cry;
A murky storm shall soon rampage by;
The structure ill-maintained;
Sorrows of the patients heightened.

-(St. Paul's Asylum; 1889)

A couple of chairs, pillows two;
The walls greyish-blue;
Lots of hanging pictures, an oak desk and bed;
The comfortable blanket, velvety and red.
Wooden floor grimy;
No residents, empty atmosphere rimy;
Partly open is the one window;
Jars, cups, bottles, plates… Slight gusts of
breeze flow.

-(Bedroom at Arles; 1889)

Hair styled fashionably;
The lady strikes the keys delicately;
Sheet music propped;
She lifted the melodies and dropped.
A candle nearby glimmers;
Orange and peach, her gown shimmers;
Notes like the tinkling of a waterfall;
The hums of the piano beckon and call.

-(Marguerite Gachet at the Piano; 1890)

A firmament overcast, mauve and pink;
The lanes…. down they sink;
Indigo-roofed cottages with towering trees
behind;
Despondent rain-clouds glide.
Unkempt gardens at the rickety gate;
Untrimmed ferns coil and mate;
Chimneys pewter with smoke;
In this land, serene are the folk.

-(Thatched Cottages in Auvers; 1890)

EDOUARD MANET

Black hair, black beard, suit of black;
A thick tome he peruses, straight is his back;
Plenty of parchment stacked;
A feathery quill, inkpot old, white and cracked.
Mahogany desktop, chestnut walls;
Pictures of white blossoms and a bird that calls;
Skin fair, a stern look;
Upon the table, a leather-bound book.

-(Portrait of Emile Zola; 1868)

Silvery, satin garbs against a darkened, gloomy
room;
Irises in a pot bloom;
Folded fan in hand, a lady sits;
Within the crook of another's arm, a green
umbrella fits.
A navy blue tie around the man's neck;
Pantry in the backdrop, a coppery fleck;
The doors green, the three gaze;
Bathed they are in the afternoon's daze.

-(The Balcony; 1868)

Skin like the last layer of winter's snow;
Her long skirts… silvery-blue they glow;
A snug boudoir, duvet with pillows white,
green;
Stockings of silk, a pretty sheen.
Hair piled over her head, golden;
A wood drawer from days olden;
Mirror with candles on each end;
A picture of a bird with its neck craned.

-(Nana; 1877)

A cap and a blue dress, the lady plump;
Leaves in a vase… a clump;
Against the table, a young man leans;
Tobacco blown out of a pipe, the maid cleans.
Food still not touched, wine and meat;
The wall onyx, for a dining room, 'tis unfit;
At the corner, a middle-aged man reposes;
As he exhales, the vision closes.

-(Luncheon in the Studio;1868)

Spice-flavoured and strong;
Clouded fluid and wrong;
Waiting in a goblet to be gulped by the man;
His shadow wan.
A bottle carelessly thrown;
Touching the ground, the pieces of glass groan;
A tall hat, black boots, in brown he's clothed;
The sickly green liquid frothed.

-(The Absinthe Drinker; 1859)

Rifles held up to the chest;
The trigger is pressed;
Fumes from the shot hover in the air;
A death granted to the emperor.
Warriors six fire;
Two generals in a crisis dire;
The scent of demise;
Agonizing are the cries.

-(L'Execution de Maximilien; 1867)

Horses gallop, their riders aflame;
The winner shall rise to fame;
Cheers high from the crowd;
The hooves loud.
Brimming with excitement;
Race-ground spilling with merriment;
The hills and the trees shiver;
Preferences of the masses waver.

-(The Races at Longchamp; 1866)

A masquerade, faces unrevealed;
To the unknown, yield;
Black tailcoats swirled;
The music lovely, the dancers twirled.
Hall thriving with enigma;
Joy pours out like magma;
A feel of mystery and throbbing hearts;
The desire to unravel spurts.

-(Masked Ball at the Opera House; 1873)

Upon the river, the boat drifted;
The easel the artist lifted;
To the canvas, the waterscape is committed;
Sunlight filters not, the sky lamented.
His companion sat, watching his hued slashes;
Under the awning, the silence of the two
clashes;
The untouched, clamped oars;
Spirit of the keen painter soars.

-(Claude Monet Painting in his Studio; 1874)

A lopsided orange hat, a golden head;
The fruits he held, red;
Hands rest on wall of brick;
The sharp stems prick.
Lips curled, face scrunched in smiles;
Young eyes gleam, happy depth for miles;
Leaves enwrap the scrumptious berries;
Ripe and full, the plump cherries.

-(Boy with Cherries; 1858)

HIROAKI TAKAHASHI

As evening mist settles low;
Winds encircling fog begin to blow;
Barren boughs bent;
The illumination from the street-lamp spent.
Hazy outline of a lady through green and blue;
Sandals make a soft sound while locks flew;
The lantern in her hand penetrates the vapour;
Horizon visible through beacon of paper.

-(Geisha by Lantern-Spring Evening; Taisho
Period 1912-1926)

A crescent moon high;
Brown hills, a bridge over waters nigh;
Two men hauling a palanquin;
Sedge hats worn by their kin.
The stream ripples with shadows dark;
Orange-indigo heavens against the lunar mark;
Headed towards lit huts;
The river curls around the mountainous cuts.

-(Going Home in Sunset; Taisho Period
1912-1926)

Towards the full moon, a child gestures;
As the silhouette of a tree festers;
Yellow reflections on the lake beside;
The mother holds the boy's hand, walking
along path wide.
A man with a mule;
The cottage in the far distance where lights fuel;
Muddy embankment steep;
The night ages, folks sleep.

-(Moon Rising at Nokizaki; Shin Hanga
Period)

Bent under the downpour's dominance;
Squelching in the mud, the rickshaw wheels
prance;
With heavy steps, the driver trudges;
The dank sepia sky seems to bear grudges.
Pools of water drip down the roof of brown;
Sinking low with the cold, the thin grass blades
frown;
Trees swing dangerously;
Threatening to topple ominously.

                    -(Night Rain at Asagaya; Taisho Period
                                      1912-1926)

The low, curving bridge flecked;
With winter's late snow, 'tis caked;
Streams of rime floating atop the river;
An old woman with a cane catches the fever.
Roads swept by flakes, several layers entwining
houses;
Moon seen through mist, the ice douses;
A frozen village, white;
All chilled to the bone, the night-time frost
bright.

-(Snowy Night with Hazy Moon; Taisho
Period 1912-1926)

Like lapis lazuli is the bay;
The white sails sway;
Clouds hover near the peak so steep;
With a basket, a man traipses near the shore, not
too deep.
A red gateway;
Trees endure the harsh weathers' flay;
The backwaters encircled;
Little isles shielded.

-(Utagahama; Taisho Period 1912-1926)

A clear, dazzling day;
The afternoon in May;
Teahouse overlooking a low range;
A snack the owners arrange.
Customer single, reposes on a stool;
Shadows of the store pool;
Firs orange at the rim;
On the lake, images of clouds brim.

-(Tea Shop at Nakaizumi; Taisho Period 1912-
1926)

Ravens flap their wings;
At twilight, the dusky heaven sings;
The shrine dusted with honey shades;
Darkened trees in the eve glades.
Orange fades to yellow to midnight hue;
Green not the shrubbery, black in lieu;
Clouds like scarlet fingers;
As the sun sets , the cluster lingers.

-(Pagoda and Crows; Taisho Period 1912-
1926)

At the edge of the treacherous cliff, a house
stands;
Lonely, he stretches out his hands;
The pewter sky hides the yellow lunar orb;
The light… the sails absorb.
An inn with lamps red;
Eatery, lots of people are fed;
Trees flourish at the crook of the hills;
When the moon peers down, all stills.

-(The Moon and Mt. Ishiyama; Shin Hanga
Period)

Twisting vines green;
White interior of the flower, dots of dark blue
seen;
Tints of magenta and pink;
Together, the creepers link.
Brown pot, red pot;
Kept in the conservatory hot;
Bluish buds not yet born;
The shamrock leaves scorn.

-(Morning Glories; Taisho Period 1912-
1926)

REMBRANDT HARMENSZOON VAN RIJN

The waves open their maws;
A rampaging storm that defies all laws;
The lurching ship;
The mast they grip.
The whipping sails;
Protecting the people, the vessel fails;
The screaming ocean at early eve;
The billowing waters cleave.

-(The Storm on the Sea of Galilee; 1633)

The Professor, the doctor, tools in hands;
A prone figure atop the table… He teaches as
he stands;
A study in dissection;
Seven students in attention.
An arm split open;
Stitched back with a surgeon's weapon;
They watch, clamber, lean;
The physician's work neat and clean.

-(The Anatomy Lesson of Dr. Nicolaes
Tulp; 1632)

Clad in scarlet, her locks unfurl;
She glances down as their hands curl;
The groom holds her close;
Trailing cloak behind, brown clothes.
A shy blush;
Love blooming, lush;
Hearts beating in harmony;
No one else…. Them, only.

-(The Jewish Bride; 1665)

Overhanging autumnal leaves crisp;
Ochre forests far away, merely a wisp;
A boat upon the canal oared;
As dusk descends on the grey ford.
Sandy are the banks of the rill;
The remaining rays of the day spill;
Land darkens swift;
Crests of the water drift.

-(Landscape with a Stone Bridge; 1638)

Tiara adorned with blossoms of white and
peach;
Coppery curls, below the shoulders they reach;
A flowing gown of silk, long sleeves;
Silver folds…. A crown on her head of leaves.
A long staff she clutches;
Sprays of petals upon wood, faded blotches;
A stuffed basket behind;
Twigs and sepals twined.

-(Flora; 1634)

A winding stairway lofty;
The builder of the interior crafty;
Window gleaming gold;
The darkness in the nooks, many a story told.
Of advanced years, the man pensive;
Thoughts swirl, the material world his ideas
leave;
A fire spits in the hearth;
The rays engulf him in mirth.

-(Philosopher in Meditation; 1632)

Akin to a slaughterhouse;
Reeking of blood, a peacock and its spouse;
One bird upside-down, feet tied with rope;
The other doused in despair, without hope.
Basket of tangerines, orange;
A person watches, serene…. How strange….
Rich in tinges, the dead plumes;
Ambience macabre, horror looms.

-(Still Life with Peacocks; 1639)

Face resting on hand balled into a fist;
The girl's youth hidden in a cist;
Golden hair tied, a white cap on;
All the same are dusk and dawn.
The pantry wall black with soot;
Obeying orders, she works, mute;
A few hours of repose;
Wallowing in her daily woes.

                    -(The Kitchen Maid; 1651)

A stubborn dark sky frosted chalky grey;
Haystacks and barns cold with lack of sun ray;
Braving the chill, people up and about;
A dog follows its mistress around.
Trees merely husks;
Ignoring the cloudy biting air, villagers perform
their tasks;
Mules tethered… Men, women heavily clothed;
Bluish lips pursed from being exposed.

-(Winter Landscape; 1646)

Fortress of defence beyond a moat;
The castle high… Access only by boat;
A jade, gold twilight;
Long faded, the dominance and might.
Wooded estates close;
Splendour now cold, with time it froze;
The temporal haze dissipates;
An intimidating tower of bronze shades.

-(Landscape with Castle; 16{??})

PAUL CEZANNE

Shades of golden and mauve, a mountain tall;
A town at its feet, in greenery draped all;
Azure flecked purple;
With its villas, the valley seems to warble.
Vale adorned with jade, topaz and blue;
Shrubs and bushes, many a hue;
Swathes of farmlands;
The range embraces the dale, encircling hands.

-(Mont Sainte-Victoire seen from
Bellevue; 1895)

Hand resting on trousers brown;
A mop of golden crown;
In silken blue he's dressed;
A vermillion garb over his chest.
A cushion draped in emerald;
Heavy is the curtain, with age 'tis dulled;
Picture in the background;
A thinker, the boy…. Making no sound.

-(Boy in a Red Vest; 1889)

A sloping lane;
Leading down to the glen;
Hillocks lining either side;
The tree tall hides it from nature's remarks
snide.
The house of despair behind;
Its interior unkind;
Pale violet ranges beyond;
The dwelling cold… The townsfolk… There
exists no bond.

-(The Hanged Man's House in Auvers;
1873)

Low hills on one end;
Backwaters visible… glimmers of silver, to the
eye they send;
Clumps of bushes;
Olive and ochre, the wind pushes.
Blue as the heavens;
The roar of the cove deafens;
At noon, the seascape pleasantly bright;
Port to the left, estuary to the right.

-(The Bay of Marseille seen from
L'Estaque; 1885)

Magenta and carmine canvas;
Fruits in porcelain amidst the white crevasse;
A jar speckled red;
The flesh of plants, who shall be fed?
Scarlet wall;
Entangled tablecloths of silk fall;
Against glistening purple, tangerines rest;
The rich ripeness, flavours at their very best.

-(Apples and Oranges; 1900)

Amidst the woodlands dense;
Over the muddy waters, a bridge immense;
Trunks thin, pale green leaves;
Flora scarce jut out like eaves.
Brown reflection;
Under the truss, dark shrubs' ovation;
Criss-crossing foliage;
Growth of sage.

-(Maincy Bridge; 1879)

Mottled… Red, black;
With a slapstick, they smack;
Diamond-shaped pattern;
Face fair, the stage's lantern.
Soundless, a pantomime;
Joker's mischief, his crime;
A look of melancholy;
The lace around the neck frilly.

-(Harlequin; 1890)

Crystalline is the lake;
Image of aquamarine trees fake;
White-washed dwellings amidst the forest;
Where river-worshippers rest.
The embankment yellowed;
Firmament of afternoon mellowed;
Woods pale and sombre;
The stillness of quietude yonder.

-(Banks of the Marne; 1888)

Deck slapped on the amber table;
Cards held between calculating fingers capable;
Two hatted folks;
A pipe lets out smokes.
Clubs, diamonds, hearts, spades;
The Ace dominates;
Grey coat, yellow coat;
To the game, they devote.

-(The Card Players; 1895)

The tinkling notes softly call;
Melody like the silvery sounds of a waterfall;
The cascading tunes gentle and low;
Rivers of music flow.
The knitting girl near the performer in white;
She pays no attention, out of her sight;
Comfortable, the ambience;
The soul the tones cleanse.

-{Girl at the Piano (The Overture to
Tannhauser); 1869}

PIERRE-AUGUSTE RENOIR

Adorning the golden head, a hat with flowers many;
A little girl stands beside her sister, mood sunny;
Festivities of hues; houses, streams and vines, beyond the fence;
A basket stuffed… Vegetables, fruits, appealing to the sense;
Floral brooch, the older lass in blue and red;
The potted plants bestow them with shade.

-(Two Sisters {On the Terrace}; 1881)

Sunlight trickles down her gold hair long;
As two girls endeavour to play a song;
Poring over a sheet of notes;
The tune of the grand piano resonates in the air
and shyly floats;
Boudoir elegant, decked with heavy curtains
and a vase;
Brown against green folds, the tresses of the
other lass.

-(Girls at the Piano; 1892)

Hands around her waist;
Couples waltz at the fest;
Courting a young lady;
It isn't quite easy;
The pale pinks and purples of her pretty gown
twist;
The man in dark blue, busy as he woos…
Forgotten is the feast.

-(Dance at Bougival; 1883)

On the head an orange bow;
She seeks to water the plants low;
Small stature, a blue dress;
The shamrock garden… Around her, the plants
seem to press;
A narrow pathway;
Multicoloured tints, the breeze swirls at mid-
day.

-(A Girl with a Watering Can; 1876)

Tucked away is the inlet;
The steep cliffs violet;
Shrubbery above the rocks;
The calm waves sapphire… Sandy amber
docks;
Upon a chair, the noble woman sits;
Her hands busy as she knits.

-(By the Seashore; 1883)

Rickety fence not enough to hold back the rose
bushes;
The artist's brush swishes;
Dotted with red, the garden scarlet;
The paints yellow, green, orange, violet;
Low villas in the vicinity;
Flair flourishes not in the city.

-(Claude Monet Painting in his Garden at
Argenteuil; 1873)

Crimson hair flaming;
Ribbon of blue flying;
Hands clasped gracefully on her lap;
The bent olive leaves gently flap;
Shadows surround;
Maroon entwining scarlet at noon is the ground.

-(Portrait of Mademoiselle Irene Cahen
d'Anvers; 1880)

A thick tome of old;
Vision channelled, forgotten tale cold;
Orange cravat, a cap brown;
Perusing closely with a small frown;
Red lips pinched in distaste;
What kind of world has the author spawned,
what sort of nest?

-(The Reader; 1876)

A patterned porcelain vase spilling;
Upon the tablecloth, flowers falling;
Whorls of pink, about to blossom;
Petals dainty and white, wholesome;
Dying leaves clipped;
In water, the twigs are dipped.

-(Roses and Jasmine in a Delft Vase;
1881)

An orchestra of shades;
From pink to mauve, the sky fades;
Carmine dances with yellow;
The sloping hillocks shallow;
Brown unites with green, both dark and pale;
The vast sweeps of the dale.

-(Landscape near Cagnes-sur-Mer;
between 1908 and 1914)

EDGAR DEGAS

Pristine white frilly skirts;
Across the stern hall, each student gracefully
darts;
One foot ahead;
The left limbs of the ladies primly tread;
Not a step missed;
The dance floor… the toes kissed.

-(The Ballet Class; 1874)

Necks and backs exposed;
The ladies posed;
Ocean-blue and azure;
The performers sure;
Over corsets, the gowns trail;
They leap and twirl, eyes closed; the veterans
do not fail.

-(The Blue Dancers; 1897)

A goblet upon the table;
Sickly liquid, no golden nectar from a fable;
The woman with a silver cap ponders;
Perhaps the wine will do her wonders;
A man to her left, not many people about;
The grim diners unhappily pout.

-(In a Café; 1876)

Bales of cotton strewn about, unseemly;
Clothes displayed in shops, what transpires
behind covertly?
Sweat-drops and sighs;
Who works faster, each man vies;
A large room airy;
Garments spun, fit for a fairy.

-(A Cotton Office in New Orleans,
1873)

The store owner stitches;
Hats upon pikes' edges;
Fingers moving deftly;
Silken ribbons shaped into bows artfully;
Yellow, white, green, blue, red;
Work flawless, her hands sped.

-(The Millinery Shop; 1879)

Trumpet and cello;
The musicians follow;
Clothed in black, they gaze at the baton;
The players more nervous than they let on;
Dancers on the stage, swaying to the booming
harmony;
Not a single note out of place, ballerinas move
to the symphony.

-(The Orchestra at the Opera;
1870)

Pressing the iron hot;
Stiff is the silk cloth;
Brick walls peeling off;
Yawning…. At wealth, they scoff;
Bottle in hand, bowl beside;
Working tirelessly, dimension of hunger, thirst
wide.

-(Women Ironing; 1869)

In her hand, roses and irises;
Like a peacock, she dances;
Yellow, green gauzy skirts;
Akin to plumes…. The performer flirts;
Arms flailing with the rhythm;
Infinite talent, awed onlookers couldn't fathom.

-(Dancer with Bouquet; 1877)

Ginger tresses held;
The pull of the hair felt;
A comb was run through;
Over the months, she watched as the girl's locks
grew;
The curtains, walls vermillion;
Old, the room… Waves of time move on.

-(Combing the Hair; 1895)

Woman in red, hand outstretched;
Lamps hovering over the fair, entertainment
etched;
Spectators numerous;
The lively ambience humorous;
Jocular players, instruments strummed;
The hearts of emissaries drummed.

-(Café-Concert at Les
Ambassadeurs; 1877)

TOSHI YOSHIDA

Bamboo boughs, yellow and green like lime;
Ducks wading, the stream warbling in
pantomime;
A hut with a garden of stone;
Shrubbery tended to and grown;
Mountain draped in white;
Plum trees grey, blue in sight.

-(Bamboo-Friendly Garden;
19{??})

Overflowing with vermillion, orange and
yellow hues;
Grey mountains against the smoky blues;
Boulders encircling the pool as cascades
descend;
The stony pathways curve and bend;
Hedges near the entrance;
One cannot help but glance.

-(Autumn in Hakone Museum;
Showa Period 1926-1989)

As rain falls relentlessly;
Footfalls of two women sloppy, splashing
unceremoniously;
Parasols shielding their forms;
The heavens splattered with harbingers of
storms;
Wet streets, damp shadows;
Shelter a shop bestows.

-(Umbrella; Taisho Period 1912-
1926)

A shrine tucked away from curious, prying
eyes;
Forest of the gods, a hidden paradise;
The tree guardians grazing the heavens, birch
and oak;
An empty haven, no folk;
A sloping hill behind;
The stairway to the temple, steep and wide.

-(Sacred Grove; Taisho Period 1912-
1926)

Warehouses lining the canal;
Willows that tower over all;
Boats languid;
People at the pier unloading, single-handed;
Seeped in poverty, the dock;
Hopeful traders flock.

-(Iida Bridge; Taisho Period 1912-
1926)

Canopy of wisteria purple;
Busy hums from afar as people burble;
A bridge hemispherical and hollowed;
Shimmering images, the jade stream swallowed;
Behind pink, leaves peer;
Rays of the forenoon smear.

-(Half Moon Bridge; Taisho Period
1912-1926)

Decked with peach, a pale sky;
The wintry day dry;
A couple of cars dash;
Their headlights flash;
Tall buildings pewter in the pink of dawn;
The chills arrive along with the festive morn.

-(Morning of New Year's Day in Ginza;
Showa Period 1926-1989)

Waters flood the field, harvest-time 'tis;
Plateaux mauve, the firmament they kiss;
Farms yellow, brown barn;
Violating the surface of the lake, the winds
yearn;
Rice and grains white;
Soon to be reaped, with a scythe.

                    -(Rice Field in Suizu; Taisho Period
                                        1912-1926)

White cranes promenade in the fleeting snow;
The red speckles near their beaks aglow;
Gazing desperately at each other;
Voiceless vows to one another;
Rows of firs;
Mutual affection incurs.

-(Dance of Eternal Love; Taisho period
1912-1926)

Mountains many, the open glade;
From green to rosy red; towards the sky the
colours fade;
Houses orange, yellow, brown; here and there;
Not quite cheery at this time of the year;
Plenty of ferns at the base of the hills;
The scenery without people; everything stills.

-(Vail, Colorado; Taisho Period
1912-1926)

OTHER ARTISTS

A white dog at his feet;
Rapier tucked at the belt, sleek;
Rifle long, glove in hand;
He stands upon sandy land.
Donning hunting boots;
Cravat, vests and suits;
In anticipation of his prey;
Fully prepared under a sky bluish-grey.

-Goya (Carlos III in Hunting Costume, 1786-
1788)

Plumes upon a hat, red, blue, white;
The hilt of his blade, regal and displaying
might;
Golden lace upon the desk-top;
Black, above the scalp the mop.
Clad in colours that identify a raven;
Stance kingly, the room a gloomy haven;
The chair dully amber;
Shadows cast, the despondent floor seems to
slumber.

-Goya (Ferdinand Guillemardet, French
Ambassador to Spain; 1798)

Imprisoned one;
Her face pale and wan;
Light filters through a window small;
Illuminating the jail hall.
A silken dress of silver and white;
The morning sunny and bright;
Hands clasped around the knees;
Hopeless, near her brows the crease.

-Goya (Los Caprichos, plate 32, Por que
fue sensible; 1796-1797)

Orange sash, red skirt;
Out of the clay jar, water shall spurt;
The lady of rare beauty;
Provider of that vital liquid, the vessel hefty;
A basket she bears, carrying a cup;
Dying with thirst, they'll lap.

-Goya (La aguadora {The Water-Carrier})

Sunflowers bloom as the brushes race;
Dark akin to midnight, the vase;
Palette layered like a meadow yellowy;
Heavily lidded eyes, beard gingery;
Brown overcoat crusted with hues;
The walls, a festival of blues.

-Paul Gauguin (Portrait of Vincent Van
Gogh Painting Sunflowers, 1888)

As the sky bears rain;
Doused in ice, the pools remain;
Smoothly the boys glide, capable;
The field red with fallen maple;
One child falls, the rescuer picks up his pace;
The others gleefully race.

-Paul Gauguin (Skaters in Fredriksburg
Park; 1884)

Young trees along the edge;

The stream ripples by in a rage;

Reddish roofs, houses beyond;

The velvety banks of green called;

At their gestures, the mauve clouds gather;

The new-born herbage soft like feather.

-Paul Gauguin (The Market Gardens of
Vaugirard; 1879)

Wild geese gaze up at the blackening skies;
Towards a budding bough a bird flies;
A stork, water it drinks;
Each month, the seasonal links;
Gnarled trunk of pines;
Summits afar, the blanket of snow shines.

-Kano Eitoku (The Four Seasons; 1566)

The lunar pirouettes;
Hilly silhouettes;
Lower half of trees swathed in white, misty;
The branches overhead sway, feisty;
Fog of early dawn;
Erasing the moon, a new illumination born.

-Kaiho Yusho (Pine and Plum by
Moonlight; 15{??})

A swan glides, serene;
Crests and troughs wee, seen;
A steadied boat;
Basking in the season of abundance, the
wooden curvatures float;
Dressed in fabrics lovely;
Two ladies brighten the scene primly.

-Berthe Morisot (Summer's Day, 1879)

9 789354 462498